The Best of

Hitopdesh

Compiled by Mrs Rungeen Singh

Young Learner Publications™
G-1, Rattan Jyoti,
18, Rajendra Place,
New Delhi -110008 (INDIA)
Ph.: 25750801, 25820556
Fax: 91-11-25764396

Printed at : Kumar Offset Printers, Delhi-110092

CONTENTS

THE GOLDEN BIRD

Once upon a time there was a beautiful pond, with many golden swans, in the lavish garden of a palace.

Each month, the swans would give their golden feathers to the king who would gladly add them to his collection of beautiful things.

One day, the swans woke up in the morning to see a beautiful bird sitting by the side of the pond.

The swans were surprised to see such a beautiful bird. They looked at it with their eyes wide open, unable to believe their own eyes.

The bird had feathers of pure gold and they glistened and shone as the sunrays fell on them. The brilliance of the feathers seemed to blind the swans.

The golden bird went up to the swans and tried making friends with them. But the swans, feeling jealous of the bird, did not speak with him.

They all swam up to the old swan for his advice.

They said, "We do not want this golden bird here. He is just too beautiful."

The old swan smiled and said, "So, what is there to worry? He can stay here."

But the other swans did not listen to him and decided to call a meeting to discuss the matter.

One swan started speaking, "We have a big problem. This bird with feathers of gold can be a threat to us."

Another said, “Yes, we are allowed to live in the pond because we give golden feathers to the king.”

The first swan continued, “Now this bird with feathers of real gold has come. If he gifts his feathers to the king, then the king might not want us here anymore.”

Another swan agreed, “Then where will we go?”

“That is true,” added the first swan.

“You are right. We should do something about this bird,” nodded another swan.

They sat and thought what they should do about the bird. Finally they decided to talk to the golden bird.

The first swan went to the golden bird and began, “We just had a meeting and we have decided that you should leave our pond.”

The golden bird questioned, “Why should I leave this pond? This pond belongs to the king and anyone can stay here. You do not have any right to ask me to leave.”

The swan answered, “You don’t understand. If you stay here then what about us? We shall lose our importance.”

"What can I do about that? I am not going anywhere else," objected the bird.

They started arguing loudly, loud enough for the king's guard to rush to the pond and see what the matter was.

They saw the bird with golden feathers and rushed to the king to inform him about the strange bird and his fight with the swans.

The king got angry to hear of the fight and he commanded, "The swans don't own this pond. Catch all the swans and put them in cages."

The guards came towards the pond with many cages in their hands. The old swan saw them.

The old swan shouted, "I was telling you but you all didn't listen to me. Now fly away from this pond."

"The golden bird should go. Why should we go away?" asked the first swan angrily.

"The guards have many cages. They must be for all of us. Now let us fly away," advised the old swan.

Frightened, all the swans flew away to find another pond. They had lost their own home because they had been jealous of the new bird.

USEFUL BEAUTY

Once a peacock was very proud of his beauty. He strutted around as if he was the best of all.

Every morning, he would go to the lake and spread his colourful feathers for all to see.

He would then see himself in the water of the lake and feel very happy that he was so beautiful.

One day the peacock saw that a white crane had come to live near the same lake.

The peacock wanted the crane to look at him and admire his beauty.

So the next morning, the peacock again went to the lake to spread his feathers.

He spread his feathers and started dancing. But he saw that the crane did not even cast a glance at him because he was busy looking for food.

The peacock felt disappointed that the crane had not noticed his beautiful feathers. The proud peacock then went up to the crane.

The peacock wished him, "Good morning. I am your neighbour."

"Good morning," replied the crane.

The peacock had thought that the crane would now complement him but he didn't.

The angry peacock then commented, "You have plain white feathers. Do you feel bad that your feathers are not as beautiful as mine?"

"No," answered the crane.

"But why not?" asked the peacock, who was used to all the animals telling him that he was the most beautiful bird.

The crane remarked, "You may have beautiful feathers, but you cannot fly. What is the use of having beautiful though utterly useless feathers?"

The peacock was shocked as the crane continued, "So I think that I am better off because my feathers may be plain, but I can fly. It is not the beauty but the usefulness of the feathers that matters. You should not feel proud of them."

The peacock felt ashamed of himself for he understood that the crane was trying to say that beauty is useless without utility. He thought, “Now I will stop showing off my feathers to others.”

The peacock lowered his head and walked away. He had understood the real meaning of beauty and usefulness.

THE SACRIFICE

Once upon a time, there lived a king, who had everything, yet was unhappy.

He was worried about his son who was to become the king after him.

This prince spent all his time enjoying himself with his two friends, who too were good for nothing.

The prince did not help his father in looking after his kingdom at all.

One of his friends was the son of the prime minister. The other one was the son of the richest merchant of the kingdom.

All the three friends had a lot of money because of their fathers and did not feel the need to work to earn money.

They spent their days loitering around and making fun of others.

One day the king called the prince and said, "You are wasting your precious time in merry making. I think that you should realise your duties as a prince."

The prince felt ashamed and realised that he was actually wasting time. Now he wanted to do something.

He told his friends that he had decided to go out of his kingdom to earn money.

Both the friends also wanted to go with the prince.

The prime minister's son said, "My father too wants me to do something in life. I will come with you."

The son of the rich merchant spoke up, "My father also wants me to prove myself. I will come too."

The three friends then discussed where they should go.

The son of the merchant suggested, "Let us go to the north. In the mountains there are many gems. We can get them and sell them for a lot of money." The others agreed.

So they all went to the north. They passed the forest, crossed a river and faced many hardships before they reached the hills.

There they saw many gems and picked up a big gem each. Now they were ready to return to their city.

The son of the merchant said, "On the way back we will again have to pass through the dense forest."

"We might meet bandits or wild animals," added the prince.

"So we should break our gems and swallow the gems with fruits. Then the gems will remain safe from the robbers," said the merchant's son, unaware that a robber hiding behind a tree was listening to their conversation.

When they had finished breaking the gems and swallowing them, the robber came up to them and requested, "I am a traveller. I also have to go through the forest, but I am afraid of bandits. May I come with you please?"

The friends agreed and the four of them started walking.

As they were passing through the forest, some bandits came and surrounded them.

They were caught and taken to the leader of the bandits, who enquired, "Did you go to the north hills?"

The prince said, "Yes."

"Did you get gems with you?" asked the leader.

The prince replied, "No. You can search us if you want."

The leader answered, "That means you haven't got the gems. All right, you all can go."

They started walking away when the leader shouted, "Wait. You might have swallowed the gems."

The leader ordered his people to tie up the four of them.

The leader said to his men, "In the morning we will cut their stomachs and look for the gems."

The four were tied to trees.

The robber could not sleep and kept thinking the whole night. He felt ashamed that he had spent his life doing bad things like stealing and killing innocent people for money.

The robber really felt sorry that he had not done anything good in his life.

The next morning everyone stood around the four of them. The leader asked his people to cut the stomachs of the four young men.

The robber shouted, "I want to ask you for a last wish."

"Yes, what is your last wish?" asked the leader.

"Please cut my stomach before you do anything to these three young men," said the robber.

The prince whispered softly to him, "Why are you doing this? You don't even know us."

The robber answered, "I am a robber. I had heard you all. I wanted to steal but now that I am sure to die, I want to do something good before I die."

The three young men tried to convince the robber not to insist to get killed first but the robber would not listen to them.

The young men then said, "Thank you so much. God bless you for your sacrifice for us."

The young men felt sad as a bandit cut open the stomach of the robber. No gems were found in his stomach.

The prince and his friends were now waiting for their stomachs to be cut.

They could see death looming large before their eyes.

A bandit moved towards the prince but just then the leader said, “Leave them.”

“But why, Chief?” asked the bandit.

“These four young men were travelling together. If one does not have the gems, the others also would not have the gems. Let them go free,” ordered the leader.

This was what the robber had thought would happen when he asked to be killed first. So he had indeed saved the three friends.

The bandit untied the ropes of the three young men and they were freed.

They walked off and went straight to their city. Their families were very happy to have them back, safe and sound.

All three of them sold the gems and made a lot of money.

They gave the money to their fathers who were very proud of their sons.

Though the three friends were happy because they were alive and had come back safely, they remembered the sacrifice of the robber all their lives.

THE CATTY COUSIN

A lion was very happy with his life as the king of the forest, except for one thing.

There was a tiny mouse who used to trouble him everyday. The mouse was really very brave.

He would often climb on top of the lion when the lion was sleeping.

Sometimes he would just crawl and climb, but once he pulled off some hair from the tail of the lion. Then the lion decided that he must do something to stop the mouse.

He could have killed the mouse, but he thought, "I am the king of the forest. It would be inappropriate if I killed a tiny mouse."

The lion thought about it and then decided to call his cousin, the cat.

The lionorderedthecat,"Youstay here and it is your duty to see that the mouse does not trouble me. I will give you food daily."

So after that, whenever the mouse came to trouble the lion, the cat would chase him away.

Whenever the lion ate or slept, the cat kept guard.

In return she got very good food from the lion. The cat really loved this life.

Then one day, the lion had gone away from his cave and all was quiet. The mouse noticed this.

The mouse thought that the cat had gone out with the lion and the cave was empty.

So the mouse came out but the cat was in the cave.

The cat jumped on the mouse and killed him.

The cat thought that the lion would be very happy, so when the lion came back, the cat said, "My Lord, see I have killed the mouse. I think I deserve a reward."

The lion answered, "Why should I give you a reward? This was your duty. Go away. I don't need you any more."

"But why?" asked the cat.

The lion answered, "I called you becauseofthatmouse. Now that the mouse is dead, why should I give you food for no work?"

The cat stood shocked, feeling sad for having killed the mouse because now she would not get free food from the lion.

THE ASS AND THE DOG

An ass and a dog belonged to a washerman who was very very forgetful.

One night he went to sleep early and forgot to give food to his dog. The poor dog was very hungry for he had not eaten anything the whole day.

After some time the ass heard a noise. He woke up and saw that a thief had opened the door of the washerman's hut.

The ass saw that the dog was awake but he was quietly watching the thief.

The ass said to the dog, "You know there is a thief in our master's hut, so why are you quiet?"

"What should I do?" asked the dog.

"You should do your duty and bark so that our master comes to know that a thief is stealing his belongings," advised the ass.

"Why should I?" questioned the dog.

"He is your master and gives you food," said the ass.

The dog said, "No, he hasn't given me any food today. So I won't bark to warn him about the thief. Why should I?" The dog kept on sitting quietly.

The ass scolded him, "You should because it is your duty. You are not doing the right thing, doggy."

The dog replied, "I won't bark to warn him if he doesn't give me my dinner."

The ass became worried. The dog was being stubborn and the thief was stealing everything.

The ass could not stop himself. He started braying loudly, trying to warn his master.

The thief was angry as he thought, "Why is the ass braying? Everyone will wake up. I better run away."

The thief then picked up the belongings of the washerman and ran away from there.

By the time the master got up, the thief had run away. The master did not realise that his hut had been burgled. When he went outside he saw the ass braying.

The washerman thought that the ass was braying without any reason. He felt very angry.

He started hitting the ass.

The poor ass thought, “Men are strange. I was trying to help, but he is hitting me. The dog has not done his duty, but our master is not saying anything to him. Now I will never try to help him again.”

THE BELL GHOST

Once upon a time, a thief was not able to steal anything. He went around the village but got no chance to enter the houses.

Then he went to the temple but the doors were closed. The doors were strong and he could not break them open.

He thought about what he should do as he was very hungry. Then he saw the temple bell.

He decided to steal the temple bell and sell it in the next village.

He felt that he would get a lot of money for it, because the temple bell was very heavy.

He stole the bell and started walking over the hill towards the next village. He had to walk through a forest in the hills.

Suddenly a lion sprang upon the thief and killed him. The temple bell fell down as the lion dragged the thief away.

After a few days, two travellers were passing through the forest on their way to the village.

They saw the bones of the dead thief. Meanwhile, some monkeys had found the bell and they started ringing it.

The monkeys were having fun trying to see who could make the loudest sound with the bell.

The two travellers got scared and went running to the village, shouting, “Ghost! Ghost!”

When they reached the village, everyone asked them, “What is the matter?”

One of them said, “We saw the bones of a dead man and then the clanging of the bell started.”

The other traveller added, “It must be a ghost, otherwise how can a bell ring in the forest?”

The news spread like wildfire in the village. Everyone became afraid that there was a ghost in the forest.

All the people went to the chief of the village to inform him about the ghost.

One villager shouted, “The whole village is in danger because there is a ghost in the hills. The ghost might come to our village and harm us or our children.”

Another suggested, “I think we should leave the village and go away somewhere else.”

A woman then came and said, “I think I can free you of the ghost.” Everyone stared at her.

One villager asked, “Do you know what you are saying? Do you want to die?”

The woman replied, “I know what I am saying.”

One man enquired, “Can you really free the forest of the ghost?”

“Yes, I can. Give me some money and I will then chase the ghost away,” replied the woman.

The chief gave her the money she asked for and she went away. She bought some mangoes and then she walked to the forest.

In the forest she threw the mangoes around and then hid behind a tree.

As soon as the monkeys saw the mangoes, they dropped the bell and ran to eat them.

The woman quickly picked up the bell and went straight to the chief.

She handed him the temple bell and said, “This is the ghost.”

The village chief was very surprised. When she told him that some monkeys had been ringing this bell, he burst out laughing.

"You are very clever. You guessed correctly. You will be rewarded," declared the chief.

THE PROUD CAMEL

A poor carpenter lived with his family in a village. No matter how hard he tried, he was unable to find a job.

He did not even have the money to buy tools so that he could make things and sell them.

So he always took loans from the villagers to buy food for his wife and child.

The villagers were angry with him because he never returned the money he borrowed.

The villagers thought that the carpenter was lazy and did not want to work.

They did not try to understand that when he had no money to buy food, how could he buy tools to do his work.

The villagers just taunted him for not giving their money back. Finally, they stopped lending him any more money, and the carpenter and his family had to remain hungry.

One night, sick of their comments, the carpenter left the village while his family slept.

On the way, he saw a she-camel who had lost her way. Her baby walked behind her.

The carpenter took the two camels to his village.

From the next morning, he bathed the camels everyday and took great care of them.

He led them to the forest where they could eat grass. He took them to the pond where they could drink water.

Then he brought them back in the evening and saw that they were comfortable in the night. He began selling the she-camel's milk and started earning money.

Now that the carpenter was earning, he no longer had to borrow money from anyone in the village. The villagers too stopped taunting him. The carpenter paid back the money he owed to the villagers.

But when they saw the carpenter taking his wife and child for a camel ride then all the villagers began to feel jealous of the carpenter.

After a few months, the calf of the camel also became big and strong because the carpenter had taken good care of both the camels.

The carpenter and his family were very happy now.

Then the carpenter bought more camels and then he started selling their milk too.

The carpenter was now a rich camel trader and he continued to look after his camels well. The family was happy and content.

The villagers became very jealous of the carpenter because he was doing so well.

Once a farmer went to the carpenter who was looking for a naughty camel hiding behind some tall bushes.

The farmer advised, “You spend so much time searching for this naughty camel, why don’t you tie a bell around his neck?”

The simple carpenter did as the farmer said. Soon the naughty camel was made to wear a bell around his neck.

The camel with the bell felt that he was very special and he became very proud of himself. He felt that he was better than the other camels, so he stayed away from all of them.

The carpenter took his camels to the forest one day where he left them to graze.

The camel with the bell proudly moved away from the other camels.

A lion was nearby and when he heard the tinkle of the bell, he went to find out who was there.

He saw the camel and pounced on him. The naughty camel lost his life because of his pride.

THE FOOLISH BARBER

Once upon a time, there lived a poor man who was very clean at heart.

He was also very devoted to God and worshipped Him always.

Pleased with his prayers, God appeared before him and said, "You can ask me for a boon as you have prayed sincerely."

The man answered, "I would like to be rich forever."

God blessed him, "So be it. But you have to follow a few instructions."

God told him what to do. In the morning, the poor man followed God's instructions.

He woke up early and had a bath. He called a barber. He had his head shaved and he told the barber to go.

Unaware that the barber had not gone away but was hiding by the side of the hut, the poor man stood outside his hut as if waiting for someone, just as God had asked him to. Soon a beggar came by and begged for alms.

The poor man hit him on the head with a stick as God had told him to. The beggar turned into a gold statue which the man happily carried inside his hut.

The barber who had been hiding all this while, was amazed to see a living man turn into gold.

God had told the poor man that he could use the gold from the statue.

So the man had more money than he could spend, but he kept on praying and worshipping God.

The barber had seen how the poor man had become so rich.

The barber also wanted to become rich like him, to enjoy his life without any monetary problems. He knew that the poor man had become rich because of hitting a beggar. The barber thought that he would do what he had seen the poor man doing.

The barber went home and had a bath. Then he shaved his head. After that he took a stick and hit the first beggar who came towards his house.

But the beggar did not become a gold statue. On the other hand, blood began to ooze out from the beggar's head and he died.

The barber was caught and taken to the king who ordered him to be put to death.

Thus the greedy barber had to die because he wanted quick money, not realising that the poor man had become rich by the boon he had got from God.

THE LOYAL PRINCE

A prince came to the court of a king and pleaded, "My Lord, I want your help. I have been turned out from my kingdom."

"Why have you come here?" enquired the king.

"I have heard that you are very kind, so I felt that you will help me," said the prince.

"What can you do for me?" asked the king.

"I will be loyal to you. As I am strong and healthy, I can do any work that you want me to do," assured the prince.

"How much money would you want for your job?" asked the king.

"I want five hundred gold coins to start with," replied the prince.

"But that is too much. I am sorry but I cannot give you so much," refused the king.

"As you wish," answered the prince

and he walked away.

The prime minister said to the king, "My Lord, try this man out for a few days. We will try to find out how he uses this money."

The prince was called back.

The king said, "You can work for me. I will pay you what you want."

The king gave the prince five hundred gold coins and let him go.

He sent his men to follow the prince to see what he did with the money.

The prince first bought a small house for his wife and son. He bought some food for them.

Then he went to many temples, prayed to God and gave some money to the poor.

The men who had followed the prince told the king about whatever the prince had done.

They also told him that the prince had spent only some coins for his own needs.

Everyday the prince would go to temples and give money to the poor. He used only a little money on food for himself, his wife and his son.

The king began liking the prince because he was so honest and kind. So he appointed the prince as his personal bodyguard.

One night, as the prince was guarding the king in his room, they saw a woman crying.

The prince went to ask her why she was crying. The king also followed the prince.

The prince did not know that the king had followed him and was hiding behind the door.

"What is the matter?" enquired the prince kindly.

"I am the Goddess of Wealth. I have been ordered to go away from this kingdom. I don't want to go, that is why I am crying," said the woman.

"Why do you have to go?" asked the prince.

"I have to go because the Goddess who rules over me, has ordered me to move away from this kingdom," cried the woman.

"But the king is so good and kind. Why does she want you to go away from his kingdom?" questioned the prince.

"I don't know but I don't want to go because I like being here," sobbed the woman.

The prince asked the woman, "Can't anything be done about this? Is there no way that you can stay back in this kingdom?"

The woman was quiet. The prince looked very worried.

The prince requested, “If you go away, this kind king will become poor. Please tell me a way out of this.” The king stood behind the door, anxiously listening to their conversation.

"There is a way, but I don't think that you can do it. If you kill your son and offer him as a sacrifice to the Goddess who rules over me, then I will never have to go," answered the woman.

"I can do anything for my master. I will do it." declared the prince.

The woman went away and the prince went to his house at once. The king followed him without the prince realising it.

The prince woke up his wife and his eight year old son and told them what the Goddess had said.

Before the prince's wife could say anything, his son said, "Father, I am ready. You can sacrifice me."

The prince answered, "My son, this is what I expected of you."

Then the prince looked at his wife who also agreed, "Yes, you must sacrifice our son. Loyalty to our master comes first. He is our master and loyalty to him comes before everything, even the love for our son."

Then the prince went to the temple with his wife and son. The king followed without their knowing it. They prayed in front of the Goddess.

The prince cut off the head of his son in front of the idol of the Goddess.

Then the prince prayed, "God. I have performed my duty towards my master. Now he will always remain rich and happy. So I can die."

The prince killed himself.

His wife said, "I cannot live without my husband who was so loyal to me and to the king."

She took the sword of the prince and killed herself in the temple.

The king was dumbstruck to witness such loyalty. Tear rolled down his cheeks. He felt sorry and ashamed that someone had to die for him. He knelt before the idol of the Goddess and cried, "O Goddess! forgive me. I caused the death of this noble man and his family. I must repent for not having stopped them from killing themselves. I too must die for I have sinned. No other person can be so loyal to me as the prince. I cannot bear the burden of his death. I feel responsible for these deaths. Forgive me."

Saying this he pulled out his sword to kill himself but suddenly the Goddess appeared before him.

She commanded, “No, don’t kill yourself. I will bring these three back to life.”

As she spoke, the prince, his wife and son came back to life. The king embraced the prince and his son.

The Goddess said to the king, "You are kind yourself and the people who serve you are also very loyal. You all need to be alive to look after other people. So there is no need for you all to take your lives. I give you all my blessings."

The Goddess then disappeared from there.

The king praised the son of the prince, "You are really a good son. You were ready to die so that your father could be loyal to his master. I am proud of you."

The son replied, "I will do anything for my parents, My Lord."

The king then turned to the prince, "You had sacrificed your son for me. You are really a great person. I am really proud of you."

"It was my duty, My Lord. You are my master and I only did what a loyal servant should do," answered the prince humbly.

"No, it was great of you and your wife to sacrifice your son for the welfare of this kingdom. I will never forget it. You are my friend now. You will be the king of the other half of my kingdom," said the king.

From that day, the two kings became great friends and ruled their kingdoms very well.

THE GREEDY WOLF

A wolf was very hungry as he had got nothing to eat. Suddenly he saw two rams fighting.

These two rams would walk away from each other and then run in and crash their horns into each other.

From his experience the wolf knew that the rams would keep on fighting till one of them died.

So the wolf sat down. He waited for one of the rams to die so that he could eat the flesh. The rams continued to fight.

Soon the rams started bleeding. The smell of blood made the wolf hungrier.

The wolf kept waiting because he knew that if he went closer, then he could get squashed between the two rams.

He was hoping that one of them would die soon, so that he could have a yummy ram meal.

The rams again walked away, turned around and then rushed towards each other and butted their horns.

The wolf thought, “Now the rams have hurt each other quite a lot. One ram seems to be near his death. I should go nearer.”

The rams were so angry and busy fighting that they did not bother about the wolf. But when the wolf went nearer, the smell of blood became very strong and his mouth began to water.

Now the wolf could not stop himself. As the ram would go away from each other, the wolf would lick the blood that had fallen on the ground.

As the rams would come to bump against each other, the wolf would run away.

Then he would come back and lick up the blood that had fallen from the wounds of the two rams.

Soon the wolf forgot the danger. He greedily started lapping up the warm blood quite oblivious to the danger.

His hunger and the smell of blood, made him forget that the two rams were running towards each other again.

Suddenly he heard the loud sound of their hooves very near to him. Startled, he looked up to see the two rams rushing towards him. He tried to get away. Alas! It was too late. The two rams ran into the wolf who died at once. If only he had not been so greedy and had remained patient!

THE LION AND THE BULL

A merchant was driving his bullock cart. He was whipping both his bulls very badly because he was in a hurry to reach the city.

Suddenly one bull fell down. Fuming and cursing, he got down. And when he checked the bull, he saw that a big thorn had pierced one foot of the bull.

As the merchant was in a hurry, he removed the thorn and left that bull in the forest and went to the city with one bull.

The injured bull felt very bad that his master had left him alone in the forest when he was in pain and could not move at all.

Then he saw that there was a lot of grass in the forest, which he could eat without moving.

He thought, "Crying will not help. I must eat this grass for I have not eaten for a long time."

He sat down and started eating and then he slept. He felt lucky to be left in the forest by the merchant.

Unaware of the bull, two jackals sat nearby talking unhappily for they were very very hungry.

Both the jackals were very lazy. They did not like to hunt themselves.

They always waited for someone else to hunt and then they would eat the leftovers.

One jackal said to the other, "The king lion is angry with us. Now he will not let us share his dinner."

"See, the king lion is coming our way. He is so angry that he is coming this way, but he is not even looking at us," added the other jackal.

The king lion had eaten alone and was happy that he did not have to leave any flesh for anyone.

Now he thought that he would have water at the pond and then go and sleep.

The king lion was feeling very happy when suddenly the bull bellowed very loudly, "Mooooow. Mooooow."

The king lion had never heard a bull before because there was no bull in the forest. He wondered where the sound had come from, when the bull bellowed even more loudly.

Hearing the bull, the king lion got scared and ran away. The jackals were very amused to see the king lion running away, with fear clear on his face.

The two jackals ran after the king lion who was running very fast. As the lion went inside and sat in his den, the jackals too went in.

The king lion heaved a sigh of relief, wondering who or what had made that sound.

The jackals came inside and enquired innocently, “King Lion, why did you run away from the pond?”

“Hush! Keep quiet! Don’t tell anyone that I was afraid,” whispered the king lion.

“But why were you afraid?” said the jackals.

The king lion said, “Didn’t you hear the loud moooow?”

“Yes, we did,” agreed the jackals.

The lion said, “If the sound was so loud, the beast must be large too. Can you find out who it was?”

The jackals refused, “We are hungry. We have to look for food first.”

“Oh, I will give you food,” said the lion.

"But we have to feed all the jackals," said the other jackal.

The lion said, "Go and call all the jackals and have a feast."

The two jackals greedily ate up the flesh that the lion had given them, as the lion sat watching them gobble up.

The two jackals then called the other jackals and everyone had a feast.

After having his fill, the first jackal said to the king lion, “You don’t worry, My Lord. I will find out about the big creature.”

After they walked away from the den, the second jackal asked the first jackal, “What have you done? Why have you told the king lion about finding that thing? How will you find out about that creature?”

The first jackal smiled and replied, “Do you remember when we had a fight and I went to the village near the forest without you?”

“I remember we were all so scared for you,” replied the other jackal.

“Well, there I heard the same kind of bellow and I saw that an animal called bull makes it. The bull is a big but harmless animal. He grazes only on grass and plants,” said the first jackal.

“Oh! Is that so? So we should not be afraid,” said the second jackal happily.

"Now let us find out where the bull is and how did it come into the forest," planned the first jackal.

They saw the bull after some time and the first jackal told the other jackal, "Sit like a king's general. I will send the bull to you."

The first jackal walked up to the bull and asked, “We know that you live with humans and work for them. Why have you come to the forest?”

The bull answered, “I am sorry. I didn’t know that I was not allowed in the forest. What should I do?”

“Go to the General of the king’s army. He will tell you,” advised the first jackal.

“Please take me to him,” requested the bull.

By now the bull’s leg had stopped paining.

Scared that he was, the bull walked with the jackal to the second jackal.

The bull fell at his feet asking, “General, what should I do?”

“Go and take permission from the King Lion,” commanded the second jackal.

“He might kill me,” said the bull.

“No. He is the king of the jungle. He does not harm his guests,” replied the first jackal.

"Come with us," said both the jackals, and the bull followed them.

After walking a short distance, the two jackals and the bull reached the lion's den.

The first jackal stopped the bull and said, "Let me tell the King Lion that you want to meet him."

The jackal went in and the lion asked nervously, "Have you found out about the creature?"

"Yes, My Lord. He is very big and dangerous, but is here to meet you," replied the first jackal.

"What!" exclaimed the scared lion.

The first jackal consoled him "Don't worry. We have convinced him to be friends with you, but my brother has worked a lot for this. Can I tell him that you will give him a feast?"

"I will give all the jackals many feasts, but you must remain with me when the creature comes to meet me. Don't go away," pleaded the king lion.

The lion went out and saw the bull. The bull said, "My Lord, I want to pay my respects to you."

"But you are as mighty as me. Stay in the forest as long as you want," the king lion granted his permission to the bull though deep inside he was still feeling a bit scared.

The bull walked away happily. After that he lived in the forest as a guest of the king lion, who too started liking the bull a lot.

The jackals too had fun because everyday the king lion would feed them.

One day the king lion brought his younger brother to the bull and said, "I can trust you, Bull. Please look after my brother while I get food for him."

"But what happened to all the flesh that you got today?" asked the bull.

"The jackals eat it everyday. They have finished all the stock of food that I had," complained the king lion.

"But why do you give your food to them?" asked the bull.

The lion told the whole story and the bull said, "You should not waste anything on those jackals. They have made a fool out of you."

The younger brother of the lion said, "This bull only eats grass and will never take your food. Make him incharge of the store."

"You are right," said the king lion.

The bull was given charge of the store and the jackals were told by the lion king that they would have to take flesh from the bull.

The jackals did not like this at all. They did not like the fact that in just a few days time the king lion had become very friendly with the bull.

They were missing the lavish feasts given by the king. The bull gave them only as much flesh as was sufficient, never extra.

The first jackal complained to the second jackal, "We were having so much fun. The bull has spoilt it all."

"What can we do about it?" asked the second jackal sadly.

"We can change them from friends into enemies," answered the first jackal.

The second jackal nodded his head in agreement and said, "You are right. We have to trick both of them into believing that the other has hostile feelings towards him."

Then they started planning cunningly of how to make the bull and the lion king lose their trust in each other and turn them into bitter enemies.

The first jackal went to the lion and said, "The bull has changed. He is no longer your friend."

"I don't believe you. He is my friend," replied the king lion.

"He wants to kill you and take over your kingdom," the jackal told the lion.

"He already holds a very important position in my kingdom. I treat him as my best friend. Why would he want to become the king?" asked the surprised lion.

"He is greedy and has become your enemy," insisted the jackal.

"How do I believe you? What if you are lying?" asked the lion.

"If he comes with his horns lowered, then will you believe me?" enquired the jackal. The king lion nodded.

Then the second jackal went to the bull and said, "Run away from the forest because the king lion wants to kill you and eat your flesh."

"I don't believe you. The king lion is my friend," answered the bull.

"Would you believe me if he opens his mouth and glares at you and holds his tail stiff?" asked the jackal.

Then the second jackal ran to the lion and said, "The bull is coming to kill you."

The lion saw the bull coming towards him with his head lowered, ready to attack.

The bull saw the lion glaring at him. They forgot their friendship and charged at each other with all their might.

They both started fighting, while the jackals felt happy that they had made the two friends fight.

The bull put up a brave fight but the lion was stronger.

He attacked again and again and in the end the bull lay dead. The lion stopped suddenly ashamed of what he had done.

He hated the sight of his dear bull lying motionless on the ground covered with blood.

Suddenly he heard a funny sound.

"Hee hee hee hee!" He knew what it was. It was the laughter of the jackals because they had won. The king lion understood now. The jackals had been cunning again and had made a plan. The jackals had made him fight with his best friend, the bull.

The king lion felt very guilty wondering as to why he had trusted the cunning jackals. He was angry at himself and his stupidity. They had made him kill his own friend.

He really missed the bull and he thought, "I wish I had not believed what these jackals had said against my wonderful friend."

Feeling sad, the lion cried, "I have made a mistake and so I have lost my wonderful friend. Now I will not believe anyone till I am convinced myself."

THE LOST RAM

A ram lived in the village. He was very good looking with his white fleece and strong horns.

One day he felt bored with the village he lived in so he started roaming around.

He entered a forest where his master had never taken him and he looked around. He wandered on, marvelling at the beautiful sights in the forest.

After sometime, he turned to go back to the village, but lost his way.

He looked for a place to make his home. He chose a place where there was a lot of grass.

No animal dared to trouble the ram because no one had seen a ram before. They felt scared of the strange creature.

The curved horns of the ram and his strong and big body made everyone afraid of him.

One day the lion saw the ram hitting a tree trunk with his horns.

The lion thought, "The animal is hitting a tree and shaking it. This animal is very dangerous. I will stay away from him."

The lion ran away and after that he tried to stay away from the place where the ram lived.

One day, the lion was running after a deer to catch for a meal but in vain.

He could not catch it because the deer ran away very quickly. Then the lion had to return through the place where the ram lived. He had no choice.

The lion thought he would run away quickly before the ram could see him, but then the lion saw that the ram was eating grass and plants and not meat.

The lion thought, "This animal is not dangerous as it is eating only grass. I am feeling hungry. I could not get the deer. Let me taste the flesh of this creature."

The lion ran towards the ram who could not see the lion, as he was busy grazing on the lush green grass of the forest.

The lion pounced on the ram and quickly killed it. He ate the flesh to his heart's content wondering why he had been afraid of the harmless ram in the first place!

GOOD AND BAD

There was a shady tree by the road. A man was walking to the city nearby and he felt very tried.

So he sat down under the tree and soon dozed off.

On the tree lived a crow and a goose. They were friends and stayed together.

The goose was very kind but he did not know that the crow was very bad.

The goose saw sunlight falling on the face of the sleeping man and beads of perspiration forming on his face.

As he was kind, the goose spread his wings to block the sunlight falling on the man's face.

Unfortunately, the man did not know that the goose had been kind to him while he was sleeping.

The crow was bad. He always found a lot of pleasure in troubling others.

The crow flew and sat on a branch, right above the sleeping man. Then the crow spat on him and quickly hid behind the leafy branches.

The goose stood still, shading the man's face from the sunshine. He did not see the crow spitting on the man. The man felt something wet and sat up angrily. He looked up and saw the goose sitting on a tree branch above him. He did not see the clever crow who had hidden himself in the leafy branches. The man thought that the goose had dirtied him when he was sleeping and he picked up a stone and hit the goose.

The stone was very big and it hurt the goose badly. The surprised goose flew away screeching with pain.

The crow knew that his life was in danger too. But he kept quiet for sometime because he did not want the man to know that he too was on the tree branch.

Finally when the man sat up to eat his food, the crow flew off from the tree.

The selfish crow had caused pain to his loyal friend. He had not even bothered to come to his friend's rescue when he was in pain.

The goose would not have suffered had he been more careful while choosing a companion for himself.

VILE COMPANY

A lion killed animals for his dinner and was the first to eat the flesh of the animal he had killed.

When he finished his meal, then his three friends would eat the leftovers.

The three friends of the lion were the tiger, the jackal and the crow.

They never wanted to do any work themselves, so they fed on the food left by the lion.

To make sure that the lion would let them eat the leftover food, they would try to please the lion.

They would praise him and say that he was the best of all the animals in the forest.

The lion loved to hear this praise and so kept these three with him.

So the three became fat and lazy and the only effort they made was to keep the lion in a good mood.

One day, they saw a camel who had come into the forest from the village. The lion too was surprised to see the strange looking creature.

The lion went closer to see the hump of the strange looking animal he had never seen before.

He found the camel very queer, so he wanted to know more about the camel.

He said to the camel, “I am the king of this forest. You are welcome to stay with me in my cave.”

The camel replied, “Thank you so much. I will be true to you always.”

They all started living happily together in the cave of the lion till one day the lion fell sick.

It was also very hot. The lion became weak and could not catch animals to eat.

The tiger, the jackal and the crow were too lazy to go outside to find food and they stayed hungry too.

But the camel would go out and eat. He became healthy and strong. As a camel can live in a hot desert, the heat in the forest did not trouble him.

The crow, jackal, tiger and lion would stay hungry while the camel happily ate the green grass in the forest.

One day, the crow said to the tiger and the jackal, "See how healthy the camel is. Let us kill and eat the camel."

The tiger said, "The lion will get angry if we kill the camel."

The jackal insisted, "I think I can manage to make the lion agree."

The crow asked, "Then what are we waiting for? Let us try our luck."

They went to the lion and said, "You must be fed. We cannot see you dying of hunger."

The jackal suggested, "The best way is to feed you the camel who looks so healthy."

The lion answered, "No! The camel is my friend."

The crow remarked, "But it is his duty to keep you healthy. If he offers himself then you should kill him and eat him."

The jackal added, "Then you won't be guilty of killing a friend. You are not well and you have to eat or you will die."

The lion knew that he was very weak and so he could not hunt for food. So they started making plans together.

The crow, the jackal and the tiger then waited for the camel and got up as soon as they saw him.

They all walked to the lion and the crow said to the lion, “My Lord, I cannot see you hungry. Please kill and eat me.”

The lion replied, “No, you have been with me so long. I cannot eat you.”

The jackal volunteered, “You have given me so much love and care. Please eat me, My Lord.”

“No, I can’t. You are my friend,” answered the lion.

The tiger then insisted, “We are of the same family. You eat me so that you don’t die of hunger. It is my duty to see that you are well again.”

The lion refused, “But it is my duty to take care of you. So how can I kill you?”

The camel did not want to die but he thought that he too should offer himself to the lion. He was sure that the lion would refuse.

The camel then requested, “My Lord, you need to stay alive. So please eat me.”

At once the lion pounced on the camel and tried to kill him.

Realising the bad intentions of the lion, the camel quickly ran away. The camel was saved as the weak lion was no match to his agility. The lion lost a true friend as he let himself be misguided by the vile company he kept.

TRUE FRIENDS

A crow sat in the hollow of a tree observing all that was happening all around him in the forest.

He saw a man coming into the forest. The crow knew that he was the man who caught birds.

The crow saw the man fix his net to catch birds. The man spread some rice on the net as bait and hid behind a tree.

Some pigeons were flying over the forest. They saw the rice grains and flew down.

The pigeons wanted to eat the rice grains but their king was very wise.

The king pigeon questioned, "How can there be rice grains in a forest? Don't go near them."

"But I am hungry," insisted a pigeon.

"Don't be greedy or you will be caught. Just control yourself, we will find food somewhere else. Let us go," advised the wise king.

Other pigeons too got tempted seeing the rice grain and reluctantly the king pigeon agreed to go down with them.

As they sat to eat the rice grains, they got caught in the net.

One pigeon said, “The king told you all not to come near the grain, but you didn’t listen to him.”

They started blaming each other and then the king said, “Stop. This is not the time to blame each other. This is the time to plan our escape from this net.”

All of them started thinking and then the king pigeon saw the man coming towards them.

He shouted, “Be ready. There is danger as the birdcatcher is coming. All of us must fly off together with the net. Now.”

All the pigeons flew together and the net was carried away with them. The crow also went after them to see how they would escape from the net.

The birdcatcher ran after the pigeons but could not catch them. The pigeons had flown high enough for the birdcatcher to reach them.

The birdcatcher was fuming with anger, for he had lost not only the pigeons but his net too. He slowly walked back home.

As they were flying, the crow heard one pigeon say, "We are free of the man but how will we get out of this net?"

The pigeon king said, "The mice king is my friend and he will surely help us."

The pigeon king made the pigeons fly to the mice king who came out as soon as he saw them.

"What is the matter, friend?" asked the mice king.

"Please help us by gnawing the net," requested the pigeon king.

The mice king answered the pigeon king, "I must free you first, my friend. You are the king."

The pigeon king refused, "No, my friend. If you help my pigeons first, then I will feel happy. Kings should look after their subjects."

"I am small and weak. I may get tired by the time I free the others," warned the mice king.

"But we should think of others first," insisted the pigeon king.

As the mice king started gnawing the net, the crow thought, "The pigeon king is so noble. The mice king is so kind."

Soon the mice king freed all the pigeons. The pigeon thanked the mice king for his help and flew away.

After the pigeons had flown away, the crow went to the mice king and praised him, "I want to be your friend. You are so kind and helpful. I would very much like to be your friend."

"But you are my enemy. You always eat up mice. You might eat me up one day. How can I trust you?" asked the mice king.

"I know that, but now I promise never to eat any mouse. Now I will not eat anything at all, till you promise to be my friend," said the crow.

"Yes, I will be your friend," promised the mice king.

From that day onwards both of them stayed together. They liked each other so much that they spent the whole day together. The crow even made his nest on the same tree where the mouse lived.

Then one day the crow warned, "My friend, I will have to leave this forest because I can't find food here any more."

"My friend, I will come with you because I cannot live without you. But where will we go?" asked the mice king.

"I have another friend, the tortoise. We can go to his forest," suggested the crow. The two went to the forest of the tortoise, who greeted them very warmly.

The tortoise welcomed the crow, "It is wonderful to see you again."

"There was no food left in that forest," explained the crow.

"There is plenty of food here in this forest," assured the tortoise.

"Meet my friend, the mice king. He is very kind," introduced the crow.

"Welcome to this forest," said the tortoise and the three started living together.

They would play and eat together. They had never been happier before.

Then one day, as the three friends were playing, a beautiful deer came running towards them, looking very scared.

The tortoise asked, "What is the matter?"

"A hunter is chasing me," gasped the deer breathlessly.

"Come and sit with us. Eat something. I am going for a swim. I will be back soon," said the tortoise.

The deer was given food by the crow and the king mice. Then suddenly they heard the tortoise shout, “Help! Help!”

They ran ahead to see that the hunter had caught the tortoise. The mice king said, “We should save the tortoise.”

The crow asked, “What should we do?”

The mice king explained his plan.

The deer ran ahead and lay down on the path while the crow sat on him waiting for the hunter to come by. The moment the crow saw the hunter coming, he started pecking at the deer, pretending to scavenge the deer.

The hunter came with the tortoise and thought, “How lucky I am! I have a tortoise and now a deer is lying here.”

The hunter left the tortoise and went towards the deer. In the meanwhile, the mice king quickly nibbled the strings with which the tortoise was tied, to enable him to run away.

As the hunter neared the deer, the deer suddenly sprang up and ran away as fast as his legs could carry him. The crow too flew away.

The deer was so fast that the hunter could not catch him. The hunter went back where he had left the tied tortoise.

He said to himself, “So what if the deer has run away, I have the tortoise.”

When he came back, he saw that the tortoise had run away too. Fuming with anger at his stupidity and greed the hunter went back home disappointed and empty handed

The four friends then sat down to rest.

From that day the crow, the king mice, the tortoise and the deer became really good friends, and lived happily ever after.

BIG AND SMALL

There were many fishes in the sea. Some were big but most of them were small.

The big fish were real bullies and always troubled the small fishes.

One big fish boasted, “Everyone is afraid of us because we are the biggest and the most powerful.”

When the small fish challenged the big fish, the big fish made fun of them.

They told them, “You are so tiny. Don’t try to fight with us. We are the giants of the sea. We are so big and powerful. You all are not important.”

One day a fisherman came and he threw a net into the sea. The net was large and strong.

The big fish were caught but the small fish slipped through the holes of the net and remained free.

The small fish then laughed and said, “Being small has a lot of advantages also. Now you will become a dish for some humans while we will live and be happy here in the sea. What use was it to be big and strong when you could not save yourself from the fisherman?”

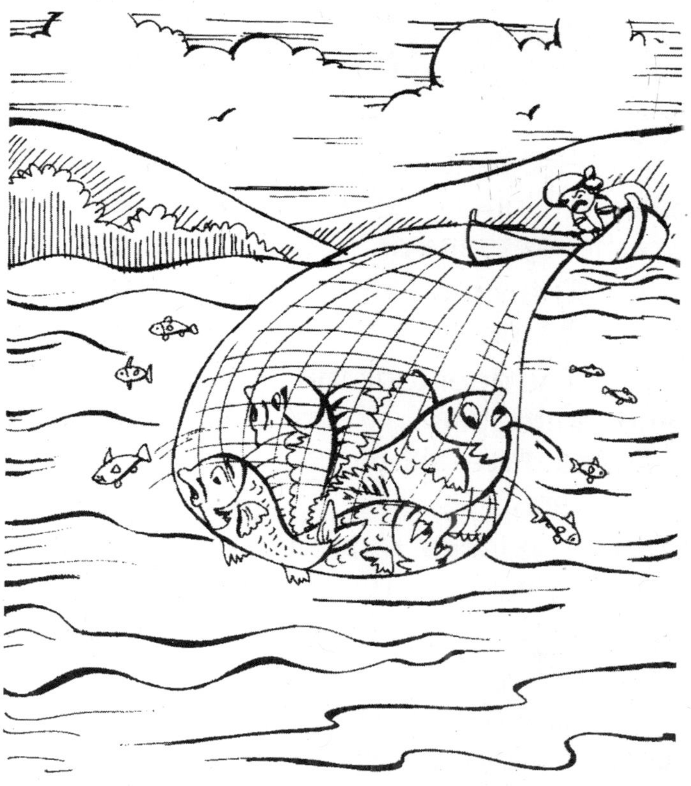

DON'T TRUST STRANGERS

A very long time ago a deer was very friendly with a crow. One day a jackal saw the deer.

The greedy jackal wanted to eat the deer. Clever that he was, he thought of a trick.

He went to the deer and asked, "I am very lonely as I have no friends. Will you be my friend?"

The simple deer agreed, "Yes, I will be your friend."

The deer took the jackal to the crow and introduced them, but the crow refused, "We should not be friendly with strangers."

The jackal reminded the crow, "The first day when you met the deer, you too were strangers, but today you are very good friends."

The deer pleaded, "Come on crow. Let us live together peacefully. The more the merrier."

The crow agreed and they began living together. They would go out separately to get food for themselves and then come back in the evening.

The jackal started taking the deer to a field of corn everyday and one day the farmer saw the deer eating the corn.

The next day the farmer spread a net and the deer got caught in the net.

The deer thought, “If my friends do not come, I will be dead.”

He saw the jackal and he became happy. He shouted, “Quick, Jacky. Get me out of this net.”

“I can’t because I have a fast today. Tomorrow I will come and free you,” answered the jackal.

The deer felt very bad. He thought, “The crow was right. I should not have trusted this stranger. He is not a true friend.”

In the meantime the crow became worried and started searching the forest for the deer.

All of a sudden he saw the deer in the net and enquired, “How did you get caught?”

The deer bent his head and said, “I should have listened to you.”

“What does that mean?” asked the puzzled crow.

The deer said, “The jackal got me into this and he refused to help me to get out of this net. He is nearby. You run away or he may harm you too.”

The crow insisted, “I will not leave you alone here no matter what happens. Now let me think of a way to save you. We must act quickly, before anyone comes.”

“Oh, you are a true friend,” smiled the deer, with tears in his eyes.

“There is no time for talk. Quick, lie down because the farmer is coming. He must have laid the net trap for you,” whispered the crow.

The deer lay down at once. He made his body stiff and he puffed his stomach out.

The farmer saw and thought that the deer was dead. He freed the deer from the net to put him in his bag.

As he took out the bag, the crow screamed, “Caw, Caw,” to signal the deer to run away.

The deer got up and ran. The farmer was too shocked to do anything at once.

Then he picked up a big stone and hit it at the running deer but the deer was very fast and the stone missed him.

Meanwhile, the jackal was coming down the path to see if the farmer had taken out the trapped deer from the net.

The stone hit the jackal who had not seen the stone being hurled by the farmer.

The jackal died and instead of the deer, the man put the jackal in his bag and went away.

From that day, the crow and the deer lived happily together again. After that the deer never trusted any stranger.

PREJUDICED VIEWS

Once upon a time a potter lived in a village. He was young and worked very hard.

He had a well built body, and looked more of a soldier than a potter.

One day he fell down and hit his head against a large stone. The fall left a deep mark on his forehead.

A few days later, his village was struck by famine. There was nothing to eat. People started going to other villages and cities.

The potter also went to a city. Unable to get any job, he joined the king's army.

One day the king came to inspect his army. He wanted to see if his army was strong and had brave soldiers or not.

He saw the tall and strong potter and felt that he must be a very brave soldier. Theking thought that a sword must have caused the mark on his forehead.

The king called each soldier turn by turn to talk to them. And then came the potter's turn. He called the potter and talked to him.

He asked, "In which battle did you hurt your forehead?"

The potter was very simple. He did not tell lies so he gave the king an honest answer.

"I fell down on the road," replied the potter.

The king scolded him, "Don't joke with me."

The potter continued, "My Lord, I have recently joined your army because of the famine. I make pots from mud and I don't know anything about war and battles."

The king became very angry. He shouted, "You have cheated me. You made me believe that you are a brave soldier."

The potter said, "I am brave and I can learn the art of fighting. I am tall and strong and I will work hard to become a good soldier."

"No, you can't become a soldier. Only those people can become good soldiers who are born into families of soldiers," the king said to the surprised potter soldier.

"You can only be a potter because you have been born into a family of potters. Get out," he shouted at the potter.

That day the king, due to his prejudiced views, lost a competent member of his army, who could have performed brave deeds on the battlefield.

THE STRANGE BOON

There was a weaver who was very good at weaving cloth. He made fine silk cloth with lovely designs and patterns, but still he was poor.

He used to go to the forest to cut wood so that his wife could cook.

One day as he was about to hit a tree with his axe, a very sweet voice said, "Please don't cut this tree. It is my home."

The weaver could not see anyone around, so he picked up his axe again to cut the tree.

Again the soft voice requested, "Please don't cut the tree."

The weaver asked, "Who are you?"

"I am the tree fairy. If you cut my tree, I will have no home left. I will grant you a boon if you don't cut this tree."

The weaver could not think of anything to ask from the tree fairy. So he said, "I shall ask my wife and then tell you."

"Take your time," said the tree fairy. The weaver ran home to ask his wife.

The weaver was running home when he met his friend who asked him why he was running.

When the weaver told him, the friend advised, “Ask the fairy to make you a king, then life will be very good for you and your family.”

The weaver said, “I will think about what you have said, but I have to ask my wife.”

Then he went home and told his wife about the tree fairy and the boon.

He told her, “My friend told me to ask the fairy to make me a king.”

“No! A king is constantly engaged in wars and has to take good care of his subjects. I don’t want you to be worried or vexed,” replied his wife.

“Then what should I ask for?” questioned the weaver.

“Let me think. I have a brilliant idea. Why don’t you ask for another head and two more hands,” suggested the wife.

“But why? What am I going to do with another head and two more hands?” asked the weaver, puzzled at what his wife had said.

"You will then be able to think of more designs and you can do more work with two more hands. So you will earn more money," said the wife to the weaver.

The weaver liked the idea and he ran back as fast as he could to the forest.

He reached the tree and then he started shouting for the tree fairy.

After sometime he heard the soft voice of the tree fairy replying to him.

The weaver said, “I have come to ask you for the boon.”

The fairy replied, “Ask me what you want and I will grant it.”

The weaver requested, “I wish that I have one more head and two more hands.”

The fairy agreed, “So be it.”

The weaver saw that he had got four hands now. He could also see more, hear more and smell more because he had two heads.

He felt very strange with the two heads and four hands, but then he remembered that this was what his wife had wanted him to have.

So he ran home to his wife but on the way people laughed at him. Children were scared of him.

Many men thought that he was a monster and threw stones at him. He had to suffer because he had not used his brains before asking for such a strange boon.

A BIRD WITH TWO HEADS

Once upon a time there lived some birds, called Bharunda birds.

They looked like cranes but had two faces, one each on two long necks attached to one body.

In the beginning there were many such birds but they slowly disappeared.

Then finally one day, only one such bird was left. This bird was searching for food.

The left head saw two berries. The left head quickly ate one of the berries, without offering it to the other head.

The right head saw the berries and requested, "Give me one berry. It looks very juicy. I also want to taste it."

But the left head refused. "I will eat both the berries because they are so sweet. And I found them. Why should I share them with you?"

The right head asked, "What about me?"

The left head said, "We have a common body. These berries will fill our common stomach."

The right head felt very bad because it wanted to taste the berries too.

The right head then wanted to teach the left head a lesson it would never forget.

The right head saw some poisonous berries. It dragged its body and the other head to the berries and ate them.

Then it told the left head, “I have eaten these poisonous berries. We have a common body and a common stomach, so you will have to suffer.”

The left head replied, “You fool. What have you done?”

“I have poisoned you,” shouted the right head.

“You have poisoned yourself too. Didn’t you think that you would also die because we have a common stomach?” asked the left head.

The right head answered, “I never thought about that. What can we do now? Please do something. I don’t want to die.”

But it was too late because the poison had spread throughout the body.

The bird with the two heads died, just because the two heads were selfish and did not care for each other.

SLEEP TALKING

A minister fixed the marriage of his beautiful daughter and planned a very grand wedding. Elaborate preparation were made and skilled cooks were called to prepare the lavish feast.

He invited the royal family to the wedding. Everything was planned well.

Soon the king came and the minister welcomed him warmly. The minister escorted the king to his seat.

The minister was shocked to see a sweeper siting on the seat specially reserved for the king.

He got very angry and shouted at the sweeper, "How dare you sit here! Get out at once."

The sweeper felt that the minister had insulted him in public. He wanted to take revenge. The wedding went off very well and everyone was happy except the sweeper.

Next morning the sweeper was cleaning the bedroom of the king and he murmured, "There is something fishy going on between the queen and the minister."

Just as the sweeper had wanted, the king heard him.

The king asked, "What were you saying?"

The sweeper replied, "I don't know, My Lord. I talk in my sleep and right now I am half asleep."

But this made the king very anxious. He wondered if what the sweeper was saying was true.

The king got so angry with his minister that he did not let him enter the court.

The minister realised that something was wrong. He was clever to guess that the king's anger was due to the sweeper.

So the next day he called the sweeper for a meal and fed him nicely with a lot of respect.

Then he said, "On the wedding day I was very tired so I screamed at you. I am sorry."

The sweeper answered, "No, I should have not used the seat meant for the king. It was my mistake."

The minister gave some gifts to the sweeper. The sweeper went away thinking, "The minister is a kind person. I should see that everything is right between the king and the minister."

Next morning the sweeper was cleaning the king's bedroom again.

The sweeper said, "There is something fishy going on between the king and the chamber maid."

The king got angry and shouted, "What are you saying?"

"I talk in my sleep, My Lord, and I am half asleep right now," answered the sweeper.

The king thought, "What the sweeper has said about me is not true. Then what he said for the minister and the queen must be wrong too. I have made such a big mistake. I must make up with the minister."

The king then ordered the minister to be called back at once to the court to work.

The minister started coming to the court again and all was well between him and the king.

THE HISSING SNAKE

In the forest there lived a long and black snake who would hiss so loudly that everyone would get scared.

He had killed so many people with his poisonous bite that no one dared to come near him.

Once a holy man came to the forest. The snake tried to bite him again and again, but the poison could not kill the holy man because he had holy powers.

The holy man spoke to the snake one day and told him that it was wrong to bite and kill other people.

The snake agreed, "Yes, I should control my anger when I feel like biting someone."

The holy man explained, "You have been born a snake because you sinned in your last birth. If you continue sinning by killing others, then you will again be born as a snake. Why don't you try to be good?"

"What should I do?" asked the snake.

"Do some good deeds so that you are not born as a snake in your next birth," said the holy man.

From that day the snake became very good. He did not bite anyone and neither did he hiss.

After an year the holy man came back. He called out to the snake who came out from his hole. The snake had wound marks all over his body and some wounds were even bleeding.

The holy man asked, “What has happened to you?”

“I have become good. I no longer hiss and bite others,” replied the snake.

“But that does not mean that you should suffer,” said the holy man.

“Earlier everyone was afraid of me because I would hiss loudly. But now they all hurt me. They throw stones at me, so I come out only in the night to search for food,” explained the snake.

The holy man said, “I told you not to bite others but I did not tell you to stop hissing loudly. You have full right to protect yourself from harm.”

“So can I hiss?” asked the snake.

The holy man said, "Yes, you can hiss as loudly as before. By not biting you are being good but you have to make sure that the people don't take advantage of your goodness."

From that day the good snake started hissing as loudly as before and nobody troubled him any more.

THE QUAIL AND THE CROW

A crow lived with a quail in a forest. They had lived a comfortable life but now their attempts to search for food often went futile.

The crow and the quail often had to remain hungry. They started thinking of new ways to get food.

One day they decided to go to the village to look for food. They flew over the road that led to the village.

They saw a man walking on the road with an earthen pot on his head.

He was a milkman who was going to sell curd in the next village.

The milkman had become very tired. He sat down under a shady tree.

The crow and the quail also sat down on a branch of the same tree. The pot was not covered and they could see the curd in it. The sight of the delicious curd began to make the crow's mouth water.

The crow flew down and sipped some curd with his beak. The curd was really sweet.

The crow did that again and again while the milkman was sleeping.

Then the milkman woke up. He picked up the pot and started walking again towards the village. The crow flew over the milkman. The quail also had to follow the crow because they were friends.

The quail did not have curd but the crow finished all the curd in the pot by the time the milkman reached the village.

When the milkman stopped, he saw that all the curd was finished.

He was really surprised and then he looked around. He could not see any child who could have been naughty.

Then he saw the crow with curd on his beak sitting alongside a quail on a wall.

The milkman became furious with the crow for having finished the curd. He looked around and saw a big stone on the ground.

The milkman threw the stone at the crow but just then the crow flew higher up and got saved but the quail could not move away in time like the crow.

The stone hit the quail and he started bleeding badly and soon fell dead.

The quail died because he had been friends with the evil and the bad crow.

THE GREEDY JACKAL

In the forest, a hunter was looking for a deer to kill, but he could not find any.

He walked on and on without realising that he had reached the middle of the dense forest.

There was danger here because there were many wild animals.

Suddenly he saw a herd of deer grazing in the forest.

He hid behind a tree and hit an arrow at one deer. His aim was so good that the arrow hit the deer straight in his heart.

The deer fell down dead and the hunter felt that all his hard work had paid off.

He ran ahead to go and pick up the dead deer. As he was running, he saw a boar.

The hunter at once took out his bow and arrow, and hit the boar straight in his heart.

The boar was hit but even with the arrow in him, the boar ran towards the hunter.

The tusks of the boar pierced the stomach of the hunter and the hunter too died. Soon after the wounded boar also fell down dead. A jackal had been watching all this.

The jackal grinned wickedly because he could see the dead bodies of the deer, the boar and the man.

The jackal thought, “I will have a very good dinner. I must also store up so that I can eat this food for many days to come.”

He started dreaming of what he would eat first. His mouth began to water at the thought of the delicious meals.

He was so happy that for some time he just smiled and laughed.

He was about to eat the hunter first when he saw the bow with which the hunter had hit his arrows.

“How lucky these men are to have these wonderful tools. Where do they get the tools from? How do they make them?” thought the jackal.

He touched the bow of the hunter and then he looked closely at the string of the bow.

“This string must be made of a sheep’s gut. It must be so tasty,” thought the jackal.

The jackal started planning, "I will eat like the rich today. First I will chew the string of the sheep's gut which will be, as starter before the main course."

He continued, “Then I will enjoy my main course. First the man and after that the boar and then the deer.

The blood can be my wine, which I will have with every course of my dinner.

This is really my lucky day today. Here let me start.”

So the jackal bit into the string of the bow. The string broke off at once.

The string pierced the mouth of the jackal, right up to his head and he died there and then.

The jackal had thought that he would have a wonderful meal and he would store for the future also, but he could not enjoy even one full meal because of his greed.

THE SELFISH PRINCES

Once upon a time there lived two prince brothers who wanted to be famous.

They wanted to become great so that people would always remember them.

"I want to be famous," said the first prince.

"I also want to be known all over the

world," added the second prince.

"What can we do to become famous?" asked the first prince.

The second suggested, "We should conquer all the kingdoms of the world."

"That is a good idea but that will not be easy. For that we need to be very strong," said the first prince.

"How can we become strong to win over the world?" asked the second prince.

"There must be a way which will help us to achieve success," spoke the first prince.

They both thought about their ambition and how they could achieve it.

Then the first prince decided, "There is one way. We must pray to God. Only God can make us strong enough to win over the whole world."

Both the princes gave up the comforts of the palace and prayed day and night in the forest. Finally God, pleased with them, appeared right in front of them.

God blessed them and said, "You both have truly devoted yourself to me. I am very happy with your worship."

Both the princes were surprised to actually see God.

"God, are you really here?" asked the first prince, blinking his eyes in disbelief.

The second prince just could not speak. He stood and stared at God.

They became so happy that they started dancing and singing holy songs.

God smiled and replied, "Yes, I have come to fulfill your wishes. You both are strong and have prayed well. I am happy with both of you. Ask for any boon and I shall grant your wish."

Hearing themselves being praised by God, the praise went to their heads and they forgot the real reason behind their prayers. The first prince mumbled, "I want to see your wife, the Goddess."

God said, "This is a strange request but as I have already promised you both, I shall call my wife here."

God had given His promise, so he asked His wife to come.

The two princes stared at the Goddess and remarked, "She is beautiful."

The first prince asked hopefully, "Can she be only for me?"

The second one interrupted, "No, she would only be for me."

God smiled and said, "She is a Goddess. She is there for everyone. Just close your eyes and you will feel that both of us are there for you."

"She is my Goddess," insisted the first prince.

"No, she is my Goddess," asserted the second prince.

"There must be a way to decide this," said the second prince.

"We are princes. The only way to decide this is to fight. Whosoever wins, the Goddess shall be on his side," suggested the first prince.

They started fighting with each other. First they hit each other with their fists. Then they took out their swords and started fighting fiercely.

The Goddess requested God, "Please stop them."

God replied, “Let them decide for themselves. They do not know that Gods and Goddesses cannot be divided.”

“But they are young and are unaware of the truth of life,” said the Goddess.

“We Gods and Goddesses are for one and everyone. I have granted their boon and now it is for them to decide what they want,” stated God.

Suddenly there was a scream and they saw that the first prince had stabbed the second prince with his sword.

Before dying, the second prince also attacked the first prince and killed him.

Both the brothers died because they had became selfish. If they had asked for the right thing, the boon of the Lord could have given them a lot of happiness and success.